Measure It

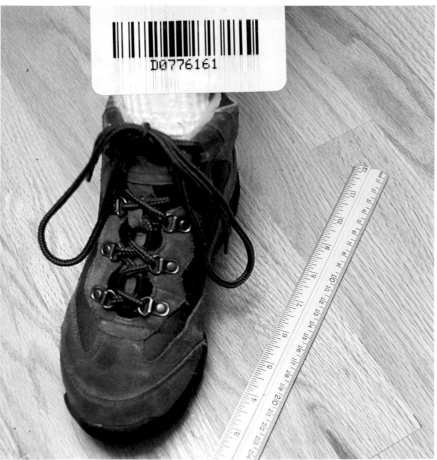

By Gloria Bancroft
Photographed by Steve Young

I use a ruler
to measure my foot.

I use a yardstick
to measure my room.

I use a tape measure
to measure the playground
4

I use a scoop
to measure the popcorn.

5

I use a spoon
to measure the oil.

I use a cup
to measure the flour.

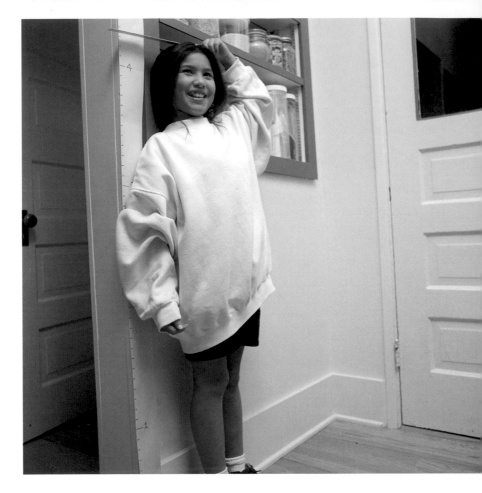

I use the wall
to measure me.